T0160297

IT'S A BIG DEAL!

ALSO BY DINA DEL BUCCHIA

*Coping with Emotions and Otters**
Blind Items
*Rom Com**
Don't Tell Me What to Do

*Published by Talonbooks

IT'S A BIG DEAL!

POEMS

Dina Del Bucchia

Talonbooks

© 2019 Dina Del Bucchia

All rights reserved. No part of this book may be reproduced, stored in a retrieval system, or transmitted, in any form or by any means, without the prior written consent of the publisher or a licence from Access Copyright (The Canadian Copyright Licensing Agency). For a copyright licence, visit accesscopyright.ca or call toll-free 1-800-893-5777.

Talonbooks
9259 Shaughnessy Street, Vancouver, British Columbia, Canada v6p 6r4
talonbooks.com

Talonbooks is located on xʷməθkʷəy̓əm, S̲k̲w̲x̲wú7mesh, and səlilwətaʔɬ Lands.

First printing: 2019

Typeset in Garamond
Printed and bound in Canada on 100% post-consumer recycled paper

Cover and interior design by andrea bennett

Talonbooks gratefully acknowledges the financial support of the Canada Council for the Arts, the Government of Canada through the Canada Book Fund, and the Province of British Columbia through the British Columbia Arts Council and the Book Publishing Tax Credit.

LIBRARY AND ARCHIVES CANADA CATALOGUING IN PUBLICATION

Del Bucchia, Dina, 1979–, author

    It's a big deal! : poems / by Dina Del Bucchia.

ISBN 978-1-77201-225-5 (SOFTCOVER)

    1. Title. 11. Title: It is a big deal!

PS8607.E48253818 2019   C811'.6   C2018-906313-0

CONTENTS

TIPS

TALK IT OUT

BIG IDEAS

MEGAFAUNA

TIPS

MARKETING

Read *Marketing for Dummies*. And then set it on fire because you are no dummy! You are a master of marketing. There are suits for that. No, not the kind you're thinking of, with their sleek lines and pockets made for patterned squares and neat hems. No. Like a superhero. That's what you could be. Walk past the suit place, the boring one with the greys and blacks and maybe a deep red, like wine or blood, but not past the custom-tailoring place. Get your whole self measured. Did you forget to bring in your custom design for a tight bodysuit + accessories costume? I sure hope not. Because the fine tailor is going to outfit you in the colours and style of your choice. Body-hugging. It must be so. And your logo, put it on there. It could be a rocket ship or a tree in full bloom or a dog barfing. It doesn't matter. That must be featured, emblazoned across your chest. And another thing: Do you have a penis? Then brand it. With a branding iron. No one will see it underneath your spandex, but do it anyway. It will be worth it because branding is what you're all about. Do you have a vagina? Don't brand it. But do brand a single breast or inner thigh. Logos on or near sex organs is the most efficient way to let your clients know that sex sells, and that you will sell their things. Do you believe in this plan? Do you believe in your sidekick, whom you don't quite appreciate enough? Do you believe in your ability to jump from tall buildings and punch bad guys with full force across a city block? Do you believe in your secret headquarters? Do you believe in powers? Do you believe in this new super-marketing-hero-persona? Develop it. Develop. Do you believe? Because if you can't sell yourself, you can't sell anything.

FASHION

Purchase one small item per week.[1]

Don't think about belts.

Never talk about waistlines.

Accessorize in the dark, turn on the lights, look in a mirror, and add one item.

Pump your fist every time you wear a scarf for non-practical purposes.

Take cues from uniforms, be inspired by the aesthetic beauty of utility.[2]

Practicality is a construct.

If you describe your body using food shapes, stop immediately.

Do not talk about the bodies of others, but you should compliment their fashion choices.

It's okay to talk about string bikinis or blinkinis.[3]

It's okay to wear swimwear, even out to dinner.

It's okay to wear a dead woman's clothes if you loved her or if she was a stranger, but not out of spite.

---

1   These could be earrings, a bracelet, a hairpin, a crop top, but never a G-string, unless it's visible above the waistband of your trousers.

2   These uniforms must not be obvious or overused in sartorial circles. Good examples include: sanitation engineer, miner (flame retardant), sandwich artist.

3   "Blinkini" is a regional term for "blink-or-you'll-miss-it" string bikinis used primarily in the Southern Interior of British Columbia.

It's okay to wear stolen clothes.[4]

It's not okay to wear only shoes.[5]

Decoration is more useful than people think.

---

4   Clothes may have been stolen from friends, lovers, ex-lovers, people you
    wanted to have sex with, people you wished you hadn't had sex with, and
    any and all retail establishments.

5   The exception: If shoes are plastic and you are wearing them in a communal
    shower to avoid foot fungus.

DIET

===

Worry about food additives you can't pronounce.

If you're worried about yeast infections make a baguette into a bikini brief.

Try foods you hated as a child and if you still don't enjoy them spit them back onto your plate.

Counting calories at formal dinners is a great way to alienate people you love.

If you eat after 9 p.m. you probably have a terrible job that forces you to work until an hour that is well past 9 p.m.[6]

Wine pairings are often a trick to get you drunk faster.

Don't use the term "mini-meal."[7]

Sleep on a waterbed filled with cooked pasta for a great night's sleep.

Think about how "protein" sounds like "pro-teen."

Dress your steak in a small basketball jersey and think about if you still want to eat it.

Eating bow-tie pasta is considered fine dining.

---

6   If you encounter this old adage about not dining late you must immediately draft an email describing what it's like to work in the service industry, detail how weekends are an illusion, and create a chart to show your distressing sleep patterns and irregular work hours. Ask those with the time to write *HuffPo* diet pieces if they get home on shaky transit at 11 p.m. and can barely lift a cracker to their faces, if they now have to wake up at 6 a.m. to do it all over again?

7   Those who use the term "mini-meal" are often found to have committed petty crimes of the heart.

Keep a food diary wherein you confess only your unbidden love of certain foods.[8]

Measure out a full one hundred percent of daily fibre and slowly snort it during the day.[9]

Never know your accurate weight, but merely guess and write it on the wall in your kitchen weekly.

Free pour your spices.

Keep all candy refrigerated.

---

8   Hide this diary in your underwear drawer like any self-respecting diarist would do.

9   This method of fibre intake ensures a one-minute maximum pooping time.

FUN

Play Nintendo for at least two weeks straight.

Do not leave your home.

Do not change your clothes.

Do not contemplate what you're not doing.

Focus.

Maintain a steady grip on the controller.

Allow yourself one minute every four hours to rotate your wrists, to stare into the dusty corner of the room.

Change games every six hours.

Maintain a sturdy grudge against a single character for the duration of gaming.

Release your feelings of guilt.

Ask yourself questions:

Should I order a pizza?

Will I ever make it to the next level?

What does productivity look like?

Does Mario worry about being a plumber?

No, he jumps on turtles and flames his balls with Bowser's breath and welcomes Princess as romantic partner, as racing opponent, as a smart, independent royal.

His life is fraught with danger.

Even though it doesn't apply in this situation, repeat to yourself: "UP, UP, DOWN, DOWN, LEFT, RIGHT, LEFT, RIGHT, B, A, B, A, START."[10]

---

10   Also, "SELECT, START" is acceptable if you want to share.

LIFESTYLE

Pay someone to curate a lifestyle site for you.

You can run it or read it.

You can eat it or smoke it.

It tastes like something good for you, chia seeds or rubber.

Your lifestyle will not be called into question.

Admit you remember that type of small dishtowel from the '80s.

Don't open your mouth or your wallet.

Stare at the screen until your eyeballs just FIZZZZZZZZ, a flicker like a mouse glitch.

Rob a bank and buy the cream with the crushed-up diamonds to make your face a sparkly, exfoliated epidermis-less exoskeleton.

Or steal the cream. Or convince a cute teen to steal it. The important thing is to have it.

Read the lifestyle site and admire the lifestyle site and life choices even though you cannot afford to read it.

You can barely afford to look at it.

Do you have hundreds of hundreds? No? Then look away. Shut it down. Throw your computer through the window.

Rescue your computer, look at the many pieces scattered on the sidewalk.

What kind of life did this computer have?

What kind of life will it lead now that it's broken, that you damaged it?

Repair the computer with something ineffectual: duct tape, eyelash glue, Hubba Bubba.

Take photos of this decrepit computer, glue a wig to it, add a fake nose, rip the eyes from your childhood stuffed toy.

Photos are meant to be studied.

But other things will be called into question and you will have to answer for them.[11]

---

11 I.e., What year did you purchase this computer? Where did you purchase this computer? What brand of clothing were you wearing at the time of the purchase? Do you carry your money in a wallet, or willy-nilly in your pocket? Have you ever played the lottery? Just scratch tickets, pull tabs, or Lotto Max? Gambled? Blackjack, poker, one-armed bandits? Told someone how you really felt? Have you ever felt like a winner?

TRAVEL

Open an Instagram account.

Master Photoshop.

Stay home.

HEALTH

Make a list. Of every specific date that you felt your healthiest. Don't forget the month, day, year. If you can remember down to the hour this will be one of your healthiest moments, a sturdy building block toward future health. But first, go back. As far back as you can and try to remember the first time you heard the word "healthy." Who said it? A smug pediatrician? Your parents in unison after you'd eaten a bowl of expired candy and a glue stick? A classmate who only ever brought whole foods for lunch, who'd never wrapped a fruit roll up around a finger, sucked, and slurped? Think more. At a standing desk take three to four hours and write out the definition of health. Edit and re-edit. It should come from deep inside you. But also, it should come from research. Journals, medical books, blogs written by people with no background in studying science, health, or the human body. Do not write down a dictionary definition. This will damage your health centre. If you try and take a nap during this process it will completely reverse the benefits of any previous work and you will have to begin again. Never sit. Unless you're perched on an exercise ball and you are in perfect alignment with the universe and you can't think any thoughts because you've gone so far back into your consciousness that you've ceased being a physical being at all. Once you've become a putrid vapour, then you'll achieve maximum health and exhale yourself into the ether.

CAREER

Roll up your sleeves. Finding meaningful work is about getting dirty. Headaches will develop, that's part of unemployment and partial employment. You are a part of the gig economy and you can't tune an instrument. If you've ever filled out an aptitude test shred it, then burn it, then scatter the ash in a glass of seltzer and drink it. This isn't so you'll absorb it, but so you can get those ideas out of you. Right answers are like trick questions. Focus on the thing you love. What gives you happiness? What brings basketfuls of fulfillment? Now look at the average salary of a person who does whatever that thing is. If it makes you faint or cry out like a newborn piglet, then you don't need to make a pros and cons list. You are not ready for a career based on love. Not everything can be your dream job. Sometimes you need to have a few nightmares, be shaken awake by the thunder of fear. Think back on something that made you feel okay, that you are good enough at. Enough. Enough. Enough. It sounds like heavy breathing. The mark of hard work.

FINANCIAL

Think of your financial situation like the tips of your nails. The way they shine after a manicure, buff out the rough patches, pluck ragged cuticles, paint colour over basic, chipped keratin. Get ahead by investing in yourself, in the beauty of this part of you that you use every day. Shake hands and impress. Hold out to display a ring. Fingers reach into a wallet and then out to pay with cash or credit. Nails always visible.

An investment.

A manicure costs $12 or $28 or $60. An amount you can afford. Gels, fills, glue. You decide. Only you can decide what you can afford.

But it's hard to maintain. Chips, breaks, colour clashes. You have to reinvest. Make trips to be foiled, acetone eats away. But you pay, put in that investment, that time. You've worked hard. You decide what you can afford to pay to put up with who you are.

The Vietnamese woman scrubbing your hungover hands wears a paper mask against chemicals that break down deep colour. But when you pay she breathes in the night of Long Island Iced Teas perfuming your skin.

You're not breathing the same air. You don't even have the vocabulary to describe the scent in this room.

When you walk out the door your nails will clack against a keyboard in an air-controlled room or tap out annoyance at the checkout of the organic market or rest against your sides as you hope someone notices your effort in financial planning. Like flashing freshly minted loonies.

But you didn't get the fancier option. Wanted to save a little money. Without an upgrade the sheen dulls.

Not so special now.

They were on special.

You paid for those. Selected "Savings."[12]

---

12   You are saved.

PRO

It's considered pro if you approve a document with a large rubber stamp.

Don't concern yourself with business casual anything.[13]

If you fake it till you make it you will in fact become unnaturally, truthfully phony.

Every hashtag is an opportunity to make others feel shame or nausea.

Sarcasm becomes you about ⅛th of the time.

The charming, harshly beautiful woman you know from grad school is a master of sarcasm and can get away with it 90% of the time, you on the other hand are the opposite.

To appear balanced, mix your numerical measurements.[14]

To be thought of as super professional, declare it on your website.[15]

---

13   This will only insult you and others.

14   This can be done in a recipe.

15   This can be done in a few simple clicks, and total commitment.

HOUSEHOLD

Work too much, collapse in bed, worry about bills and relationships and that shirt you shouldn't have bought, and then you'll forget to eat dinner.[16]

Don't have children.[17]

Not enough people ask the right questions about household tips. For one, how do you make your household sexier? The answer is to masturbate in the linen closet. But also keep a floral sachet in there.

A stud finder is not a joke.

Save the rubber bands that come with your bánh mìs. Use them to keep your plastic spoons and forks from rattling around in your junk drawer.[18]

If you must dust underneath the narrowest crevice, then use the cheap lace underwear you were hoping would make you feel more beautiful.

Cut up your credit card to prevent further debt. These shards can also be used to spear pickles or cheese cubes at a very casual get-together.

A glamorous way to display your refuse is in a regular garbage can, decorated with the scarves you thought would add a jaunty flavour to your look.[19]

---

16   These are great ways to save money on meals.

17   Another great money-saving solution! Probably the top tip for any household looking to save.

18   These serve as a reminder of the irreversible damage of plastic.

19   Though they are not sentient, you know this is your way of punishing the scarves for not quite working out the way you'd planned.

DATING

As soon as you admit things to yourself it's simple for them to slip out to someone else.[20]

Research and write an essay about the word "date."[21]

Subscribe to *Cosmo* and *Maxim*, but do not read a single issue. They just need to be on your credit card bill. This is called a "dating credit score."[22]

If you're at a restaurant with a white tablecloth, flip over your table before you're seated. This will show your date that you identify with the little people.

Don't trust anyone who uses the phrase, "Innocent before proven guilty."

Never have sex on the first date.[23]

Talk about your exes, but as if they are ghosts that haunt you biweekly.

---

20 This will make you undesirable.

21 This includes but is not limited to the super chewy fruit and anything related to calendars.

22 This is very unrelated to an actual credit score.

23 Exceptions to this rule are:
- If it's a full moon.
- If you have had a single very dry cider.
- If the person is wearing a jaunty scarf of any kind.
- If you just really, really feel like it.
- If they smell of your childhood clubhouse.

You will get better results if you pick someone up at a mall rather than at a strip mall.

If you get anxious, wear sunglasses from the dollar store until you're comfortable with the other person.[24]

---

24 If you never become comfortable you won't feel bad just throwing out those sunglasses after the break-up, since you only paid a dollar for them.

BEATY

Brutality is a way of seeing.

Surgery isn't always the answer.

But if you pay for something it carries more weight.

Body hair rages on, no matter how you try to prevent it from reappearing.

A squid can colour your hair, but only if you let it invade your hair.

Every squid has special powers and means of controlling the feminine beauty complex.

Rub a hand along your shin to determine how much shaving one razor will measure.

Daily yoga gives your face the texture of a kangaroo's foot pad.

Even Miss Piggy was fired.

Even though Miss Piggy was fired she hiked her skirts back up over her felted legs and broke through the ceiling with her snout.

Too much importance is put onto noses.

Looking good doesn't mean you're vapid or unintelligent or important or worthy.

"Looking good" is not defined in any dictionary.

SPORTS

Only watch the halftime show.

ADVICE

Wear something comfortable for you.[25]

Speak when spoken to.

Do not go in unsolicited.

Read body language.[26]

Never say, "You people."

Never say, "Your people."

Never say, "When I was your age."

Never say, "Never."[27]

Do not clear your throat: this intimidates and can cause a mirroring effect in the throat of the advisee, which in turn can cause a *Stomp*-like reverberation that builds to a small earthquake.

For best accuracy, be a witch.

---

25 This could be anything from sweatpants, to a catsuit, leggings and a novelty T-shirt, a breezy sundress, your ex's favourite snowsuit, etc.

26 If someone looks nervous, do not raise your voice. If they are rolling around on the floor screaming, "STOP! FOR THE LOVE OF ALL THINGS, STOP!" then walk away. Likely you will not be able to speak to this person again.

27 "Never" may be used if referencing either Justin Bieber's song "Never Say Never" or the documentary about him of the same name.

TALK IT OUT

ARE YOU FUCKING KIDDING ME?

We were supposed to meet on time. We were supposed to free our minds on the sidewalk near the yoga place, but not go inside. We were supposed to. We were supposed to stop picking our teeth when out at dinner, even fast-food dining. We were supposed to secretly make wallet-sized photos. The dusk sky barely makes you remember that day when the air was on our side. Are you fucking kidding me? Were you fucking kidding me? We were supposed to make pumpkin spice latte muffins. We were supposed to look out for fails. We were supposed to make a birdhouse out of stolen crutches. We were supposed to hate this feeling. We were supposed to say, "I love you." Are you fucking kidding me?

IT'S A BIG DEAL!

Like collars in the '70s,
when we were still small,
like breaking curfew,

like silicone vs. saline.
The kind of boobs
we thought we'd grow.

Like a sale,
but not
on anything you want.

The debates online
after the debates are over
but no one stops talking.

Like holding your breath
underwater until you want
to smash your own face.

Like that time
you grammar-shamed me
when my grandma died.

And I just
had to deal.

REMEMBER WHEN

We pulled up and rolled in. We kept that matchbook for no damn good reason. The lights changed colour in the sky because of fireworks far away, the boat was rusty, the box of tampons was left on top of the canopy. Remember when leaves were a multifunctional saviour, when we didn't have enough money to care. Remember when "Symphony of Destruction" was huge?

*

Remember when that night was epic and I threw up twice and came back to party.

*

You held my hair and another time me when I couldn't stop crying about that boy I barely loved.

*

Remember how we were too chicken to get matching tramp stamps, too cool to get BFF necklaces.

*

I still remember your mom's phone number.

*

We moved, created new shapes. Texted, talked to mutuals more than each other. Realized that shared spaces are memories, place the only commonality.

*

You figured it out, learned on the job, made a career that made enough money. I kept all my eggs in a flimsy basket.

*

Remember how I would always break things accidentally? Inside running joke.

*

You asked me what my life would look like after I lost my job. Because, you said, I had no skills.

*

Remember imagination.

*

It was going to be fine. We floated, kept it together. I made hundreds of thousands. I sold the movie rights to our kitchen conversation. I bought a boat and reanimated an extinct cat. Remember? No. You don't. Because I made it up so I could keep going.

BOYS WILL BE BOYS

Okay, or
entitled little shits

until taught
not to throw

sand, "bitch,"
direct punches.

A catchphrase
can be cute,

explain away
aggression, catcalling, rape.

Blame, "can't help themselves."
Try putting other

words there, say,
"choice," say "can help themselves."

Don't say, "not all."
Don't be boring:

I don't want to hear
about our vigilance.

Raise boys
to be conscious,

to be ashamed
that they've coerced.

IT'S A THING

It doesn't matter
what it used to be,
even if it was a space
for us to think, a mess
of scarves that became
a blanket that became
a haven. An idea

we worshipped in error
to avoid learning anything
other than confirmation
bias. A thought can change,
a trend bursts from a headline,
animals grow into memes.
But can we stop?

No. Now, it's a thing.
Whatever you're holding,
dreaming, fretting over.
It's big. It towers
and sways. A microcosm
always runs the risk
of becoming a thing.

I THINK I SPEAK
FOR ALL OF US

I hate
how much
I love you.

YOU HAVEN'T LIVED

Until you've had
a baby, been lost
in newborn eyes,
pupils a wilderness,
dark trees and beasts.
Realized your limit
of personal space.
Melded bone and skin
spawned organ meat.
Stopped using the term
"That's offensive."
Sucked marrow
from the bone
of a still
breathing wildebeest.
Held the northern lights
against an icy backdrop.
Felt a rainbow
penetrate your elbow.
Worn a pair
of two-hundred-year-old
jeans. Released
helium-filled stuffed toys
at a child's funeral.
Experienced and tweeted
gratitude. Been the subject
of a controversial documentary.

PICK YOUR BATTLES

I.

You can pick your friends
and you can pick your nose
and you can probably pick your friend's nose.

2.

"I choose you!" they shout
at their Pokémon. Cute hybrids
that fight in bright animation.

3.

It gets easier.
A root canal becomes regular,
wards off evil plaque, gingivitis.

4.

You don't have
to argue. Stay quiet.
Ignore to avoid.

5.

Don't interrupt a server
at work to tell her
that her shirt is too low-cut.

6.

Call out racist comments
even if it's your aunt
who's been alive since 1933.

7.

When he brushes your thigh,
smile. A lie
to get bigger tips.

8.

In the lunchroom talk to your co-worker
who is obsessed with cars,
to avoid the one who farts.

9.

Hum, sigh,
try every flavour of gelato
while a line blooms behind you.

10.

Don't pull yourself
together just because
someone told you to calm down.

WOW! YOU'VE CHANGED

You've changed.

You used to be so

and now you're all

like, you've transformed

I don't know how to describe

it's like

you don't like canasta anymore

you text IN ALL CAPS

your selfies are so

animalistic

like, are you out to prove something

you're a lion

you're a bear

you're a maggot

you're a virus

I just don't know

if we can be friends anymore.

PAY ATTENTION

Follow along. There is no choice when someone narrates themselves. They are going to that bathroom, picking up a piece of garbage, pouring juice into a glass, telling you that they are talking to themselves when really they are lying. They are narrating.

"I'm going to have some juice.

I'm going to eat a chip.

I'm going to walk three paces to the right.

I'm going to sit down for a minute.

I'm going to wave to you.

I'm going to put this box in the fridge.

I'm going to take that bottle out of the fridge."

You'll get the clearest picture ever. These simple tasks not scary, not surprising. Being done. With a voice-over, over, over, over, over.

JUST

No big deal, unless it's just what you needed. Someone you love will find a way to diminish the pleasure of a cheap can of beer. In the '80s you were supposed to do it. But with caveats: safety, a condom, a net, a breathing apparatus. I read an article about overuse of the word. It advised using it less frequently, cutting it out. Except the versatility keeps the old chestnut fresh. Joining a sentence to keep judgment at bay, or to better judge the woman in the office who rolls her *R*'s in a rasp after announcing she's eaten a croissant. Just bearable, just a pastry, just a brief break from work, just the right amount of disdain to get you to love yourself. To be fair, I've never eaten just one.

WHATEVER

We can all only care so much. Life is not a garden party. Some people live in dank apartments with not even a Juliet balcony, some people grow rows of roses in a yard with a pool and a hot tub. At different times both will be featured in photo spreads in *Dwell* magazine. Trends make room for every style. Mould can grow in so many moist places. Bed bugs, ants, and fruit flies don't examine décor, aren't size queens about square footage, don't use that to gauge which living rooms are best for infestations. Our brains fill with fear as we compare papers and sheets. I've spent an evening in bed worried I've offended a friend, a person I respect, but monsters plead not guilty because they have money to hire lawyers to badger, further harass victims. Some things should matter more. The crooked turns of phrase that end in whatever.

SORRY NOT SORRY

I felt so distressed
that I had to tell you
about the way I feel
because I'm in such
a pitiful state
really heart-rending.
If I'm being honest
I want your forgiveness
so I can sleep at night.
I've had insomnia since
that thing and now
I'm kind of pissed.
Cleanse me of my sins.
Is this overwrought?
Don't answer that!
Can I mention what it was?
Relive that action
every time I say
the word "sorry."
The more sarcastic
version of "whatever."

I KNOW, RIGHT?

I'm scared to make a list of things I know. Because either it will be too short, or it will be too revealing. Yes, I know about *Pretty Little Liars*. So what? Yes, I know about *Sweet Valley High*, and lip gloss, and which celebrity is dating another celebrity. I know ignoring racism and sexual assault makes people pieces of shit. No, I don't know as much about history. The basics. Dudes got angry, other dudes wanted power. There were dude wars. The details often feel insignificant. Not like accessories on a plain outfit. Those jazz it up. No, I don't know about car engines, or retirement plans. It's all right. I know about feelings. That women were thrown under a lot of proverbial busses for those bro wars. That cars aren't people, don't love you back. I don't always know how I feel, if I've spent enough time thinking about my mistakes, if I gave your opinion a chance. If it really was an opinion worth considering at all. If you're a shitty person, I don't want to know you. Right.

THROW AROUND (HERO)

We throw around words. Like
"hero," when no one

flies into explosions,
emerges with beautiful

bodies in hand. Idealized
valour. Bravery is a woman

not shaving her pubes
over summer. Maybe?

How do we decide?
People sign up to fight

or use medicine to save lives.
Scientific stuff. Soldiers

also, kind of murder.
It's murky. Not like a woman

using all her strength and more
to lift a car off her own

endangered child.
Not even considering

the word "super," defined
it could be just the male

lead in a movie, novel, life. Okay,
but it's also a term for a fully

stuffed, delicious sandwich.
A sandwich is noble.

Bread-hugging vitamins
and nutrients, could also

probably keep kids from
doing heroin, stick

our loved ones with sodium
and iron, vitamin C. Vegetables

would make great heroes. In their
shiny, colourful skins. Tight

as spandex they swoop down
our throats. Fresh from that

hoagie bread. Keep us
alive, feeling fresh.

CAN I SAY SOMETHING?

He spoke in a haughty breath.
A tonal misdemeanor. Hardened
consonants. *You're always crying. You're always
saying you hate something. You're always.*
So many ways to use a word. *We'll always
love each other. We'll always be together. Won't we?*
Ask a question and alleviate
blame. I'm sure certain people
ache to be told what to do
and how. Stand stiff, straight
wait to find out who they are
to other people, small blots on a page,
large spills that overtake. It always feels
like the beginning is smooth and clean,
like, I always knew what to say or was
always easily forgiven. I always say
what I almost mean, almost always
keep enough pieces of me just for myself.

ALL JOKING ASIDE

Put it away. This is not the right time for a good time. We are having a serious discussion about traditional values, about saving ourselves from enjoying life. If you put it aside it's easier. Really. It's like we're real people. I will not make fun of the size of any part of your body. All of it needs to go away. If we leave some behind it will spark, it could sparkle. It could take up space and then we'd have to get another California Closets organizer to keep track of everything. Slip it into a drawer, a lock box, an old ice cream tub. Once it's aside we can get to the real meat. Tear into topics with our teeth, the meat of life dripping in sugary ketchup, a dollop of mayo. Joking is the side dish and it's optional. At some restaurants you have to pay extra for it. When your laughter gets shushed at a casual bistro you'll know you've been asking for someone to confiscate your joking. Keep it in an office drawer like you're in trouble with the Vice Principal. That's the level of seriousness. You will need to win it back, but you won't. It will be claimed missing. You've lost. After it's aside you're trapped, you're held accountable for being fun at one time. All joking aside is on a bumper sticker from the '90s and now everyone respects it like it's in the *New York Times*. In all seriousness, I crept up on you because it's funny to scare people.

TOO MUCH
INFORMATION

It's exhausting that other people
have experiences. Instead, they
could stay silent, creep around
and listen, or stay still and wait
until I'm finished talking about
the cream soup I ate for lunch
two weeks ago, the soft leather
jacket I owned in 1998. All the while
make a list of conversation
pieces, your life, how you feel
ignored, the spike in your lower back
when you look back on your last
relationship, how you held back
so many times, a story about redemption
and the leather jacket you owned in 2003.
And in that moment as I take a long
breath, attempt to get in, but I
move on, explode with verbiage
because I don't want to know
what happens when I stop talking.

MAYBE I'M JUST USED TO IT

That smell that's not
a real smell, that's what
I've put on it.
A singular nagging,

a hemorrhoid that burrows
and protrudes intermittently.

Scald on the gum
from rushing, desiring
to taste Orange Pekoe.

Saying no, saying, It's not
like that, saying, I'm trying,
to be richer, better, someone.

When I sit in front of the shine
of black television, cross my feet,
forget time, the weight
of a wallet. Never knowing

if I'll experience
prolonged happiness. Nights
on an old couch being drunk
in love. All past. Nice memories

for an early nostalgist. I missed
being a kid at fifteen. Not clear-eyed
about romanticizing the past. I want
because it's comfortable,

unachievable.
Where is the time machine?

A vegetarian missing the taste
of a real hot dog, made of the real
grossest parts. Who misses
being surprised by
the tragedy of meat?

A girl
in denim overalls listed:
pig ears, pig feet, pig eyes,
pig assholes.

Comfortable, like T-shirts
slept into soft thinness.

A nest of feelings if you don't
know what else there is –
a mansion with a maid
to pick up after you – but then

you wouldn't ride transit for hours,
work retail, walk in the door,
and look at every mess as more work
before more work. Cleaning is a privilege,

but it's fucking detestable. You might
not dream of being tucked in at night.
Staring at a neon clock. In your real-bed,
somewhat-clean sheets. Used to falling asleep,

drool accumulated on your pillow.
Soggy nights. Maybe I just miss
being happy with you.

URGENT!

From: dinadelbucchia@important.com
To: Important Team Group Team
Attachments: grossbeheading2.gif

February 1, 2015, at 4:48 a.m.

This message is urgent.

I mean URGENT.

But really URGENT!

To add urgency, I've added a gif of a beheading. Danger lives in the subject line.

Please respond ASAP. Deadlines loom.

From: dinadelbucchia@important.com
To: Important Team Group Team
Attachments: grossbeheading2.gif

February 1, 2015, at 4:53 a.m.

The previous email was so insensitive that this new message is marked MORE URGENT because it is an apology email. It is very urgent. The original email is still URGENT! Reply now.

From: dinadelbucchia@important.com
To: Important Team Group Team
Attachments: grossbeheading2.gif, sorrypanda.gif

February 1, 2015, at 4:57 a.m.

Fwd: SORRYSORRYSORRYSORRYURGENTSORRY!!!!!!!

From: dinadelbucchia@important.com
To: Important Team Group Team
Attachments: grossbeheading2.gif, sorrypanda.gif,
forgivenessslothandmonkey.jpg

February 1, 2015, at 4:59 a.m.

Fwd: !!
!!!
!!!

From: dinadelbucchia@important.com
To: Important Team Group Team
Attachments: grossbeheading2.gif, sorrypanda.gif,
forgivenessslothandmonkey.jpg

February 1, 2015, at 5:03 a.m.

There is no security on this message because of the level of URGENCY.
You will likely receive some very devious viruses as a result, but the
most important thing here is that you and all recipients are aware of the
URGENCY.

Bcc is a tool for fools when URGENCY is involved and therefore that dirtbag who spies on you in the upstairs women's washroom now has your new secret email included in this URGENT message. If you URGENTLY need a new email address please fill out the form on the home intranet page and one will be provided for you in 2–3 days. I hope no one is stalked during that time period.

From: dinadelbucchia@important.com
To: Important Team Group Team
Attachments: grossbeheading2.gif, sorrypanda.gif, forgivenessslothandmonkey.jpg

February 1, 2015, at 5:04 a.m.

This has been a test.

From: dinadelbucchia@important.com
To: Important Team Group Team
Attachments: grossbeheading2.gif, sorrypanda.gif, forgivenessslothandmonkey.jpg, jokesquirrel.gif

February 1, 2015, at 5:07 a.m.

Just kidding. It's all very real. And very URGENT.

If you had come to the meeting on Friday instead of taking off early that afternoon to take your child to the dentist, you would be more aware of this URGENCY.

From: dinadelbucchia@important.com
To: Important Team Group Team
Attachments: grossbeheading2.gif, sorrypanda.gif,
forgivenessslothandmonkey.jpg, jokesquirrel.gif, oopskitten05.gif

February 1, 2015, at 5:15 a.m.

I forgot to send the Doodle poll link.

https://doodle.com/poll/vm6ih2es39wzf5pc

URGENT!

Dina Del Bucchia
Team Captain
Team Important
URGENT MATTERS MEDIA
Unit #1 – 1 Important Plaza
Urgent, B.C. v6g u8g
dinadelbucchia@important.com
1-800-2-urgent, ext. 1

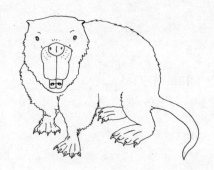

BIG IDEAS

NEW RULES

Oh shit, it's not okay.

Please don't.

Broken dreams are adorable.

Failure is self-care.

Be mindful or get fucking punched.

Don't confess your love to me.

"Cleanse" is not a noun.

Unsolicited advice is verbal garbage.

Take care of your butt.

If your instincts are to debase, then they are not to be trusted.

Don't worry about being loud.

Don't worry about being quiet.

Whispering is still and always will be rude.

Don't touch.

Believe women.

Develop deserving enemies.

Stay off the defensive.

Admit your wrongs, even silently.

Do not keep me in your prayers.

Re-examine the reasons you feel sorry for people.

Politeness is not friendliness.

REAL*

Real people

Real friends

Real world

Real housewives

Real estate

Real fans

Real women

Real curves

Real curveballs

Real balls

Real fake balls

---

* Things that exist.

SUCCESS

You can measure it. I'm sure of it. In your bank account, in your Facebook friend count, on a scale. You can hold a sack of jewels, a beautiful baby made for commercials. How young can you start measuring? *You're in the top percentile for infants. Best motor skills. Best hand-eye coordination.* In the morning you can brush your teeth, buff your skin, and login. You have fifty new LinkedIn connections today, you have a dozen new job listings, you have been endorsed for your endorsement skills. It all adds up. There are so many ways to achieve. Maybe it's a signature suit, a fragrance. How about a cold medication that works? But who will hold your head when you cry with the first blush of fever? Your hair when you barf? Who will cradle your heart in a metaphoric sling when everyone else has somewhere better to be? When the wind whips your hair into your eyes as you drive a new convertible, who is riding shotgun? Who says, with gentle concern, "Slow down, buddy!"

PERFECTION

Reflexes like a cheetah when you call or ask or don't say anything. She favourites all your less-than-stellar tweets. She watches sports with a quiet reverence and only speaks about the game when she has something truly great to say or to agree with you or when spoken to. She eats hot dogs and hamburgers, dozens of them, thousands of them, and gains no weight, no she loses weight, no she floats away like a kite you thought was really cool in 1992. She is making progress on dinner and also she makes beer fly out of her vagina and then with sex magic it's lubed up for you to fuck her. She is perfect. She is funny, talks about farts, but doesn't fart like a real person, perfumed air drifts out on a blue cloud, not a pink cloud because you hate pink and she is perfect.

POLITICS

I read a thing and posted a thing online because I only believe this thing about that thing.

The first Google image if you search "Politics" is a big, very ugly word cloud.

You never see an elephant humping a donkey.

Or a donkey humping an elephant.

Animals exert their power in humps, which is why political parties have animal symbols.

Why don't Canadian political parties have cute animal mascots?

This is the reason your family hates you.

If you bring this up at a formal function there's less chance of a fist fight.

Don't make it a thing.

Take it personally.

DEATH

Don't take this lightly.
Or do. Be callous.
People that you love
are not around.
I am always killing
plants. Which is awful.
Mostly because I want
them around to look
pretty, I want living, breathing,
attractive companions. Like
Hugh Hefner, but for succulents.

LOVE/YES/NO

Do you like me?

☐ Yes
☐ No

Fold over once and put back on my desk.

Do you like me–like me?

☐ Yes
☐ No

Fold over twice and put on the chair of my desk.

Do you like Cheez Whiz?

☐ Yes
☐ No

Fold once. Turn over. Give back to me outside the cafeteria. I'll wait.

Also.

If the answer is yes: Cool. I have some great ideas for a picnic.

If the answer is no: Me neither. I never eat it with a spoon while watching *Power Rangers* after school when other kids are hanging out beside the drained outdoor pool.

Do you like the feeling of Cheez Whiz between your toes?

☐ Yes
☐ No

Fold into the shape of a heart, decorate with purple or blue sparkles or sparkle pens. Write my initials on the back side and bury it in the flower box on Mrs. _____'s window ledge.

Did you not get my previous note?

☐ Yes
☐ No

Fold into the shape of the small intestine (duodenum). Dip into the remaining puce-coloured Trix milk for 8–10 minutes. Seal in a sandwich bag. Wrap in classy birthday wrapping paper with a curled ribbon. Do not add a bow. Leave in the broken vice on the north side of the wood shop.

Did you not realize there is a timeline on this?

☐ Yes
☐ No

Crumple this paper into a ball. Unfold. Recrumple. Unfold. Recrumple. This is the shape, texture, and feeling of my heart. If you hold it near your chest, you will feel beats. Try and make yours beat in time with mine for three days. Leave the crumpled ball on top of my locker.

Do you believe in time?

☐ Yes
☐ No

Eat this paper. Chew it up until the mulch slops down your throat and activates your gag reflex.

You do not need to give this paper back to me. I'll know what I need to know.

Do you want to go out?

☐ Yes
☐ No

Tear into thin, airy strips. Release these tassels of paper into the wind. They will find me.

P.S. I think we should go to the arcade.

P.P.S. If you want to make out sometime please seal a new piece of paper with Cheez Whiz.

CULTURE

Old things, beautiful. Curves in buildings, in women's bodies in oil paint, in language translated from some version of English to modern English. We analyze through new lenses, see the gaps, criticize for better understanding.

Now we can't avoid culture. Which is refreshing. We run into it daily, a brick wall of culture. Someone creates something every second. This typing is a song now.

We also can't avoid backlash, ageism, racism, sexism. We can't avoid deniers, people who can't bear to avoid things they don't like. A comment section run with hollow ideas about what is good according to something as narrow as a pinhole.

I think sometimes we're scared the culture police will come to our door. White men in T-shirts, who will try to take away our reality TV, who will force us to listen to something called Wilco, or the Smiths, who will diminish the writing of Carole King, pretend Rihanna doesn't exist, and try to explain away Jimmy Page's pedophilia.

On YouTube you can watch a topless child pick up a dead squirrel and laugh about it, be disturbed about, be entertained about it for years.

Somewhere, somehow the culture we love will go pop, but not in a good way, not in the way that makes our hearts swell with helium, voices high with thrill.

RESPECT

Billboards disrespect. Giddy faces,
oversized nostrils sell beige vacation
condos, candy-sheen cars. The promise
of teeth whitened without cost, without pain.

Pass in a crowded bus, with people without any
of those things. Ripped faux leather
purse soggy on the rubber floor.
Rain pools into indoor puddles, domesticated wildness.

Next block, another billboard. You ride in one.
Order food for delivery from it, but then you
have your life on view, once you get home.
Eat whatever you want, but it's a flicker

for the delivery man: dust, frayed armchair, shoe pile.
All your belongings spread and sad.

MINDFULNESS

You lying next to me,
in chronic pain,
the neighbour laughing,
music streaking through walls
into my ears, as I try to keep
it together. Your body
twitches beside me,
as you rub aching gluteals.
You croak.
Exhale. A younger you
would have joked
about me throwing
my body against the wall
to compete. You would
have walked over to ask
them to turn it down. As party sounds
die down the sounds of
barnyard fucking ramp up. You sigh.
I worry that dude is throwing
her through the wall, as my lipsticks
rattle on the dresser, as cartons
of glass seem to smash
on their floor with every buck.
She moans, and moans.
Our bed groans as I slump
into my pillow.
You moan, exhale
And somewhere between
4:30 and 6:30 I stop being
able to tell the difference
between her moans of pleasure
and your heartbreaking groans

and I wonder if this is what's
encouraged, what people
mean when they talk about
mindfulness.

RELIGION

It's nice to believe. When I was a kid I believed that bad things only lived in closets, under beds. In daylight nothing could harm. That being a girl was great, not worrying about money.

I admire gold diggers more than entrepreneurs. They have to work harder, smarter. They start from the bottom. Women make 70% less than men anyway. And that's just white women, the vipers of the women food chain. Believe it. So it's a viable option, a smart life decision to trade woman stuff for money. Bodies are multifaceted. Elbows can prop a gold digger's chin after a long night. Arms can bare tattoos that remind a woman of who she is, and who she used to be.

I believe 60% of bosses are shitty anyway. It's not really that hard to believe. At one job I had five bosses and three were fired at once for their inability to see their own shittiness. Or maybe they had faith that their shittiness would remain shrouded forever.

I have faith in the ability of people to eventually have empathy.

I believe in life after love. Because love sometimes isn't very interesting and there has to be something better than that. Life. I believe in Cher.

Belief in my astrological sign has lead me down the path of loudness and roars and a silky mane.

It's nice to have something to believe in, to feel a pulse in your chest.

I believe we're wrong so often we turn our heads to face belief so we don't cry eyes raw into our bare forearms.

CONFIDENCE

You're probably doing everything fine.
Likely, you are winning at games you play with yourself.
In the bar you are the most eligible,
playing the field means nothing, because you're a champion.
Everyone can hear you roar from the mountaintop.
You crush opponents:
you corner that woman,
call her a girl,
push your hand between the fabric
of her skirt and shirt,
open a gap.
You never question superiority.
You talk about innocent until proven guilty.
You talk about meritocracy
as though it's common practice,
as if qualifications are gospel, honest
barometers of hiring practices.
You peacock in a fedora, in a Hawaiian shirt,
in a fucking polo shirt the colour of salmon.
You consider not eating because it's not
Ocean Wise™, because you
can afford to be conscious
of your conscience.
You walk into a room,
assume heads don't turn
because of jealousy.
Hold your head on your neck,
a pedestal,
like it was sculpted from
that video for "Hello"
by Lionel Ritche.
Admirers all around.

You've never said, "Haters gonna hate,"
because you've never thought for a moment
that anyone didn't adore you.

PEACE

A hacker named Peace sold passwords on the dark web. Set up shop with millions of accounts, from MySpace, Twitter, and Tumblr. Memes and gifs and #tbts under attack. Satisfaction guaranteed. Encrypted and anonymous, unlike other image-centric titans online. Peace is one of the ugliest Google image searches with the most disappointing results. Is this why peace is so elusive? Algorithms don't make it seem very inspiring. Computer-generated tie-dye on everything. Clip-art symbols in black and white. What looks like Mickey Mouse's gloved hand with two fingers in the air. A cartoon Ringo Starr in a purple jacket and sunglasses. The world as a heart, as two awkward hands, as a dove being scorched by the sun. Doves, doves, doves. All the worst possible graphic design. Yoga in what looks like a burning field, the flames of peace coming to sacrifice all those who attempt downward dog. Economy, marketing: these don't factor into the peace equation. These images are not designed to sell. Not even a fucking sunset? A beautiful snowscape? How can hope stay in our rainbow hearts if Google doesn't think we deserve even the most basic photographic clichés?

WAR

It's good to think about teens. The way they wage war, factions crop up like weeds on opposite ends of the parking lot / school grounds. There's never money involved. Boys pummel each other on parking-lot pavement. Girls pummel each other in the locker room. Attacks involve using the word "slut" in so many ways that it starts to carry more meanings. Money is not what it's about. It's barely about belief. Feelings. Hurt feelings, deep cuts and who said what and how can we make them pay and when. Cruelty is currency. They take their developing bodies through rug burns and nude photos and accusatory Snapchats and near-sexual encounters interrupted and date rapes and insults they've just learned exist. And fear. These little wars of fear. About the present, who's in charge, and the past and what kicked anger into high gear and the future and who will take over. Boys looking up to adult incels, lying about their age to ingest knowledge about how to be better misogynists, punish girls for having choice. Involuntary celibacy is another way of saying, hey I have a boner and I am angry and lazy and I deeply hope to never understand why. Small battles over small things that escalate and roll until they're grown and have to look at themselves reflected in a 24-hour cycle so similar to scrolling through newsfeeds.

PLASTIC SURGERY

You need to mean it. And even if you don't, you need to own it. Make it yours. Whatever it is. New nose, new cheeks. You bought it. You own it.

People switch fabric swatches, paint, gussy. You do you.

I don't want surgery, even if it's necessary, so I'm sure as hell too scared to get elective surgery.

Augmentation sounds really fancy and technical and like something that should happen to more parts of life.

The term is all-encompassing.

Does it seem cool to be anti–plastic surgery? It's not.

Someone is making fun of your natural face right now too.

That's the fucking tragedy of it all.

MARRIAGE

*Marriage is a big deal, but who's to say I'm not going to pull
a Vegas and get married to see what it's like for a minute?*

—Lindsay Lohan

Rings seal deals, licence signed
before the honeymoon. Traditional

trips to relish another's body,
food you'll never eat again

if you're cooking at home.
Before that, celebrate:

toss rice, blow bubbles
for love, for life, or at least

until divorce. But then,
it doesn't have to end.

Don't let stigma stop you:
get married again! People

are prone to collections.
Collect spouses. Document

marriages with dedication: photos,
mementos, a string of URLs

for family and friends to look back
on, for you to maintain with rigorous

attention. Spreadsheets full of stats,
love levels, marriage milestones, wedding

highlights, nuptial listicles. You
can achieve at least two or three

viral wedding party videos. Ceremonial
choreography, a semi-famous singer

as ringer to heighten production value.
A professional editor, soundtrack intact.

No one can call you a hoarder,
because the world loves love.

PUBES

for Alana Green

All the colours
of a neutral rainbow!

Vajazzled to perfection
like Jennifer Love Hewitt.

Some are shaped like shorts,
or groomed into a favourite

animal, a special
memory, a historical scene.

A message in a bottle
of pube bleach

being sent to Pube Beach,
a land of curls and swirls.

Please send back a postcard
confirming you are still hairy.

Dyed to reveal
preference, a treasure map.

Shaved into notes
after each encounter:

It was okay.
This is who I am, okay?

Don't hurt yourself.
Don't pressure yourself.

I don't love you.
You were fine or whatever.

Nothing can take
up too much space

unless you use
a magnifying glass

which I imagine
you might.

Crowns of thorns
in what Mary Magdalene

would have shown
Jesus, if they

had been caught
unaware in a cave.

Rooting for meaning
in the dead strands.

We all strive to remove,
to attract and normalize.

Everything is art
nowadays, except

a strong growth,
stories in fur.

FLAVOUR

We try to taste
personalities.
Roll tongues, inhale
rogue traces.
Develop palates.

She is the salty one
because she doesn't like
being told her life
experience is invalid.

She is sweet, eats
white sugar and honey,
knows to let
a person alone
when a phase has broken.

She is bitter. Kept it up out of love,
because love is not a saviour,
because after
the honeymoon phase
there are complicated people
underneath sweaty sheets.

PRIDE

Sometimes it seems easier for every person close to me to be gone than for them to have to put up with me as a disappointment. Pressure when I think about a family gathering, attempts to careen conversation topics into things I excel at. Avoid eye contact when the future is brought up. Unless it's theoretical: talk of spaceships, technological innovations, our bodies transcending shape and space. Humans considering retirement, balancing accounts. Who will take care of my parents when I'm working seven minimum-wage jobs? If we can preserve brains by then, I will sit in virtual reality and hold their hands, make them laugh with stories about my life. Continue to avoid eye contact, wherever their eyes might be out in space. I don't need them to be proud of me, cheers and air horns. I just need to feel them pull away from their own worry. Hot chest, hands, eyes, feet. Mine still firmly rooted on the earth.

TECHNOLOGY

Inventors might be smug. A person
might develop new modes for seeing
where people are at any given moment.

A machine that hugs cows. That already exists.
Thanks to Temple Grandin. But nothing
that replicates being significant to others –

a glow from inside, a metaphor, a warm
hand to a chest. A closed-eye reading
of another's wants. We pine and wait.

Who are these people? Some of them
wear sweatpants and some wear lab coats
and very few smoke, but weed is edible now.

I guess we can call them dreamers, but
do we really want to? I hurry up and get
to curing all the cancers already, and also

prioritize a household machine
that makes peanut butter cups. But first
cancer, eviscerated. Every kind. Obviously.

Ugh. Bathing is complicated. Can it come in a pill?
Can everything just come in pill form now?
I'm not even going to say please.

RAGE

My rage cheers me up, warms me when temperatures drop. It motivates me when I think I could nap. I don't know what I would do without it? I probably wouldn't have clean sheets, or clean dishes, or any domestic chores done, ever. I wouldn't have any friends. It would be a hard life.

When I feel lonely, I can count on my rage to be my companion. We go to movies together, eat popcorn and share the armrest. Because we're not raging at each other. The movie is terrible and together we flip out once the credits have rolled. How dare they?

On a wet day in January rage settles around my body, amps up the anger that doesn't seethe enough. An electric blanket, it vibrates, I vibrate. Together, both nestled and furious, we dream our rage dreams, shock ourselves with detailed plots for how to move on.

FAME

The girl who got everyone to call you Cross-Eyed Chrissy, a freak, a sasquatch, she had to see you in black and white above the ads for used tractors and rejected pit bulls. And as you sink into your tiny tub between jobs you imagine her face, in shock that you made yourself known, surprised that you didn't climb atop the bridge to stare at your domain, crawl underneath, and live like the troll she believes you to be. And as you do tear the legs from a pigeon, tear feathers before you crunch into bones and flesh, you have that photo, that article, that image of you holding the attention of so many people who you assume didn't think you'd make it, thought for sure you were *a loser with dreams so far out of their own stratosphere it's actually kind of sad.* And he meant it. And she meant it. They meant it. But you're alive, and you paid a friend's friend who is trying to get their portfolio together to make you into a famous goddess, and you've got the laminated newsprint to prove it.

MEGAFAUNA

EXTINCT MEGAFAUNA: AN INTRODUCTION

Criteria:

1. Must be heavier than 100 lb.
2. Must be fauna.
3. Must be extinct.

These are animals that only exist as bones and casts of bones. They can't tell us anything. Not with words. Whatever we have to say might as well be true. Skulls travel in different compartments from femurs or tusks. Sometimes they take different cars, a divorced couple that gets breathing room for a time before they have to come together after a long journey. Because it would be rude not to be present together at a big event, like their daughter's wedding, or the opening of a museum in their name.

GIANT BEAVER

Castoroides

This is not a joke for frat parties. Though
I'm sure beavers still liked to have a good time.

Taller than any basketball player,
beasts with wide tails, a big, floppy booty you might say.

The broad teeth on that beaver could rip off a man's dick,
you might say. You might say the look

of these beavers' unkempt fur is retro, or disgusting.
They should have gotten a wax, gnawed off the excess.

Oh, you're really saying something. They're not around anymore.
Maybe extinct because of those jokes.

Killed by you all not being funny.

JEFFERSON'S
GROUND SLOTH

Megalonyx jeffersonii

An American founding deadbeat dad thought, maybe, there were still ground sloths lying about, stripping leaves in the Midwest. "Hey Meriwether," he said, "keep your eyes peeled for a sloth, okay? I'd kill for one." Paced the White House, arranged sloth bones along the oval carpet. Meanwhile, you hadn't been keeping it casual Friday every day for nine thousand years. You disappeared a few years after humans showed up. They were entranced. You were so meaty. Some scientists believe climate change decimated populations. It seems most sensible that murder and weather joined forces to ruin beautiful things. Jefferson stalked then married his name to you. Never one for assholes, you wouldn't have been interested. Lewis and Clark came back without you. Obsessives should keep their distance. Take it from you, stay chill.

MASTODON

Mammut

To confuse a mastodon with a mammoth is worse than extinction – it's an insult. You had a capacity for empathy, a calm way of keeping in the forest. Mammoths barged, got in other megafauna's business. You smoothed the north, took pride in grooming the landscape. Your fur shorn (less majestic you admit) than a mammoth. Bodies more normalized to modern eyes. Everyone wants to think mastodons and mammoths were related to keep it simple. Both were big, traversed grasslands, grazed for salad. Mastodons earnest, mammoths bold. With your trunk you would pluck a blossom, rescue a kitten, stroke heads to soothe sorrow.

WOOLLY MAMMOTH

Mammuthus primigenius

They trundled,
the old ladies who
refuse to use wheelie
shopping carts,
carry their groceries
in flimsy plastic,
food dangling from their bodies.

A full purse hung
from each curved tusk.
That's how mammoths
would carry all of their
hard candies, prescription boxes,
lightly used tissues.

Mammoths loved
giving unsolicited advice.

Their fur would make a terrible sweater.
Gummed up with plant gunk,
dusty and matted.
Nothing glamorous,
nothing substantial,
after clipping the knots out.

A tusk measures age
and power. Their structure
so obvious, coiled until
they point at each other,
self-referential. Comparatively,

females had much thinner tusks.
Of course they did.
Pleistocene oppression.

Imagine an old lady
stabbing you with her cane.
That's tusk envy.

NORTH AMERICAN
SHORT-FACED BEAR

Arctodus spp.

Over hundreds of thousands of years, notes scratched in caves, notepads, scribbles in the margins. So many people have commented on your face. Like graffiti on a bathroom wall, "Short-faced bear is ugly." At least you didn't have to read mean tweets on talk shows about your short face and stumpy nose. I know there are records of people calling you a butterface. Why is it always about appearance? About size? Your legs so long. Why does no one comment on that? On how fast you could run to catch and take down prey? Wild horses couldn't drag themselves away from your jaws, snapping into their spindly legs like Pocky sticks, torsos oozing like a Cadbury Creme Egg. Probably they left that out of your name because you're also top-heavy. It took so long for someone to say, "All bodies are beautiful." One of the largest carnivorous land mammals, they say. People say a lot of things. I bet you knew how to accessorize. I bet you didn't judge the other bears. I bet you had some nice friends. I bet you were fun at parties. Hauling up on your hind legs to imitate humans. That brought the house down. A short face makes for a great human impression. I bet the other bears admired your face, laughed alongside you. I bet you were a winner.

SABRE-TOOTHED SALMON

Oncorhynchus rastrosus

Fangs, like sparkly vampires,
but longer, sharper.
More in tune with rage.
Fangs.
For fighting with men
over women,
like Miocene bar bros
stabbing each other
at the end of a long night
of binge drinking.
Anadromous, only getting
their spawn on, their fight on,
in fresh water.
Keeping it chill in the salty sea.
Fierceness of fish,
who don't know
it's all about personality.
Use teeth to stab,
but only when it comes to lust,
to procreate
before extinction.
Not that it mattered much,
their machismo,
their journey to the spawning grounds,
their nightclub riverbeds
ended in their deaths.

Just a few last-minute scrapes
and cuts before
their red bodies
floated along the surface.

HELL PIGS

Entelodontidae

Top-pitch squeal,
jaws mashed,
and cheekbones sculpted,
so deadly.

On *National Geographic*
they said,
"Battle-tank body ...
bear-pig-hyena."

You were a hybrid
before science
was making DNA fluffs
into hypoallergenic pets.

But you were
no one anyone
would have wanted
to take home.

No living relatives
now. It was just you
living in extinct hell.

Worse than regular hell,
full of only the most obscure
ragged beasts. Hardcore, so metal.

Omnivore's dilemmas:
Are you eating plants or meat?
Are you a football player?

Smashing your oblong body
into predators. An attacker
attempting to score points.

But in the end, somehow
not tough enough, aggression
is not resilience for survival.

EURASIAN CAVE LION

Panthera spelaea

Everyone is so hung up
on the sabre-toothed tiger.
As if no other cats
were on the block.

In October 2015 two cubs
discovered in a Siberian cave.
Trapped by a landslide, airless.
Their fur intact, still fluffy babies,
sharp teeth not yet impacted.
Eyes still slits, not ready for seeing.
Two lumps dug from the permafrost

Rooted in the Uyandina River, they split
their bodies and their names.
It's hard for me not to say
that Dina is the more adorable.
And likely more interesting. Poor Uyan,
the dud of the duo.

The press photographed her on a block of ice,
a glamour shot. Dina in the spotlight,
scientists awkwardly posing behind her,
only there to show off her beauty. All contrast:
ancient golden fur against black parkas.

Each one looks like a mossy rock, their
solid bodies hard but delicate. No blood
pumped through those feline veins for ten thousand years,
paws shoehorned into slim bellies.

We're always so concerned with preservation
when it comes to looks. To be able to see
these faces. "The most perfect specimens,"
is what one scientist said. Untouched by weather,
they stayed as pure as possible, no air
to spoil their whiskers.

Maybe they were waiting out
some long Siberian winter,
a lioness stashing cute cargo,
roaming the river's edge for slurping deer,
lazy horses. A skilled Arctic predator.

But their teeth, so little, not sabred
Not dangerous yet, mouths
like first-graders, full of gaps.

They know about them from cave graffiti, art,
ivory carvings, clay figurines. The older
versions of '70s panthers on coffee tables.
But these wee ones are so memeable.

And now considerations for cloning.
As if they could replicate anything
about your lives. As if your strands of DNA
were whimsical ribbons swirled into modern
newborn kittens. As if no one has ever
seen *Jurassic Park*.

SCIMITAR-TOOTHED CAT

Homotherium spp.

The kind of animal that could say, "Oh yeah, I eat mammoths for breakfast." Because they did. They were eaters. Hunters. Stylish pattern mixing in their hunting gear, their fur, spots of various sizes, striped tails. Neutral tones that would blend in equally well on the plain or as camouflage at a PTA meeting. So much khaki. The internet would have loved this feline if it were swatting antelope carcasses off a cliff, purring against the barely cold body of a mammoth. Incisors, molars designed as tools. These cats would have had their own reality show. The bloodier version of *Meerkat Manor*, a warm but firm British accent narrating their murderous attacks.

MEGALODON

Carcharocles megalodon

for Roxan Marucot

As usual, it's all about
the teeth, jaws wide open.

Your name means big tooth,
But no one knew that in the Cenozoic era.

Rumoured to have gone extinct
when your food supply declined,

too frigid for whales. Yes,
the largest animal now was a meal

for the largest predators ever.
Sixty feet and one hundred tonnes requires big feeds.

Jaws too strong for a giant turtle shell,
protective layer like snapping into

a Slim Jim. They say you're gone,
so few traces left behind, just a few of those teeth.

And yet, giant squids glop
around, evaded our gaze for ages.

It's the premise for camp, B movies
that entertain with over the top

and low-spectrum effects. But
those squid survived, animals swim

down so deep. No confirmation,
where's the proof you're all gone?

Why couldn't there be a spot
in the middle of the ocean where you still lurk?

Not that I want to put you to work, but
you could garburate some of the mess

we've made. Our barges, sunken luxuries,
plastic remnants of our coping mechanisms.

Mega cosmopolitan distribution. Fancy
like that. How could an ice age stop you?

We know more about the moon, about Mars
than the ocean. I hold out hope for a catastrophic

tsunami brought on by a frenzy, a re-entrance.
Why couldn't you still be our invisible neighbours?

GLYPTODON

=========

Glyptodon spp.

Comparisons to Volkswagen Beetles
abound in literature about their bodies.

Nothing exactly like them on earth now:
a carapace of bony scutes, like fancy shingles

adorned the rotund mound, legs like cinder blocks
propping a car. Hair spiked through those plates as they

lapped at water edges, teeth crunched plant fibres,
a burly vegetarian. And slow, restricted movement

not enough to keep big cats away. Like a VW Bug
climbing a steep hill, a crawl speed. But all jokes

aside, they carried a true weapon in back. Long tail
equipped with a mace, to club and maim.

Not so innocuous. The way aggressors can be
seemingly mild, strange, and pitiable, until

you're alone, and then they seek revenge
for slights against them, nerds gone rage-filled.

They hurl insults, try to control you
with claims of hurt feelings. But then

you turn around and there's a glyptodon,
brandishing a spiked bulb that ends up in your back.

No sense in chucking a rock, stabbing with a knife,
fighting back, or striving for revenge.

With so much personal armour
he's protected. He hurts you, but can't feel a thing.

GIANT GROUND SLOTH

Megatherium spp.

Great beast, possibly the greatest of their time. Only mammoths had a mass that showed them up. They didn't understand their size, hauled their vast shapes through lightly wooded areas, brushed against small trees with force. On hind legs always searching for something to eat, prehensile lips and slender tongue at the ready. We now know they were skilled at gift-giving too, created a staple of our generation. Their innards could handle real roughage. Avocados swallowed whole, pits and all. As they sauntered along, they shat out seeds, fostering the growth of unwarranted millennial shame. If they existed now megatherium would be a guacamole mascot. A pimpled teen in a plush, giant sloth replica handing out coupons outside the supermarket door. Their modern counterparts only poop once a week. They aren't contributing to any delicious artisanal snacks, only viral cuteness. Modern sloths still give. Their extinction left an opening for the most polarizing foodstuff of our time, avocados now trucked in vehicles that matched them in weight and height. We need to send a long overdue thank-you card. Is it wrong to suggest a toast? Without their butts would we even have brunch?

YUKON HORSE

Equus lambei

My little pony, Yukon horse
racing through the tundra,
escaping predators.

Likely tripping,
clumsy gallops. These old breeds
graceless, not like a racehorse.

A smaller version of a modern equine.
But guess what? No one really cares
because we still have so many damn horses now.

This one was not very cool. Proof:
A mummified hide is on display with patchy
white hairs, sad fur, such slim calves.

It seems cruel to say, but
during the Ice Age these animals
were as basic as they are today.

These were like the original My Little Ponies,
starring Sandy Duncan and Tony Randall!
Now we have new GMO ponies with their sweet bronies.

Animals adapt and change. Their manes
become even more neon. Their theme songs
become pop-punk songs about friendship.

This is all science. There are studies:
Big fan base, merchandise, top-quality
animation. And just one more thing!

Throughout history ponies have been gross liars.
Sharing, kindness, and friendship
aren't even really that important to them.

YUKON GIANT CAMEL

Paracamelus spp.

One hump,
but so much fuss.
Twice as tall as modern
camels. Massive
limbs, stretched spines
looking down
on everything.
Shifty eyes and fluffy bodies
on stilts. Broke the camel
family tree mould
when they found
your bones, long
legs nestled in tundra.
Proteins tested to confirm
you evolved in the Arctic,
then strutted over to Asia.
All preserved in the cold,
collagen molecules tight.
You were born in ice,
strayed to the desert
and not the other way around.
I know the western camel
probably spread rumors
that they found your toe
first. They're just common.
They're just jealous.

GASTORNIS

Gastornis spp.

Certainly that toe is enough to say, "Yep this was a great big bird."
—Jaelyn Eberle, associate professor in geological sciences,
University of Colorado Boulder, interviewed by CBC News

for Meghan Waitt

Bird bones don't hold up as well as reptile, mammal.
More fragile, a light damage destroys years of safety.

Comparisons: body of a man, head of a horse,
but nothing like a minotaur, a reverse centaur body type.

Is that desirable? This form, like a Barbie, maybe.
A bobble on a twig. How did it move, navigate, live?

A single bone, a delicate, wimpy bird toe, a start,
found in Nunavut in the '70s.

Roamed the steamy landscape of the Eocene, the northern swamp,
instead of icy plains, chill tundra. A hot zone,

home to hippos and gators. Birdbrain, we say in insult.
Well, this toe, completely ignored, a clue left to mystery.

No one cared about attachment, strained to pull things together.
And now whose brain looks small? You didn't try hard enough.

We reflect in an icy pool. Past in present. Caps melt, emaciated polar bears
sink into primitive hot tubs, as we inch forward into the future

and realize we can't prepare. The same way flightless birds
could not predict their demise, feathers floated, flew away.

Not their fault that they aren't here anymore, ours that alligators
might slink from swamp again north of the Arctic Circle.

SHASTA GROUND SLOTH

Nothrotheriops shastensis

The less famous of the ground sloths. Not like that brute
Megatherium. So all about their bodies, being huge.

But the Shasta? Well, they're famous too. How do you think
the soda got its name? Their effervescent personalities, vivacious

in their molasses moves. Yet slash of claw could cut a big cat
to the bone. At first sign of a predator they stand tall,

protest the onslaught. They get defensive, but it's okay.
After the fact lounge in long grass, rip into cacti.

They would eat anything: spicy, saucy, prickly.
Dream guests at dinner parties. They make slow digs

with prehensile tongues, mock the cats not quite quick enough
to get them with paw swipes and mad jaws.

Their ash-blond bodies loll, burst with energy
from the inside. Shasta, still a soda, less popular.

DIRE WOLF

Canis dirus

You get to be
on television now.

One of the most
popular shows. Oh,

I apologize,
it's not television:

it's HBO. Prestige
cable. So many threads

from the real world
people assume, dream

as fantasy. But you
were fierce, a living creature.

Bone bodies edged out
of La Brea and

four hundred skulls displayed
on the museum wall

3D posters advertise
your sharp teeth, curved skull

the way you could
intimidate with only

a glancing blow, tip
a smaller mammal

into the black. Gas
bubbles burble.

Like a trap set for warring
factions, sticky deep

covered in leaves, twigs,
fur from another victim.

You were so thirsty.
I apologize, so hungry.

Trapped by tar while
feasting on animals

already stuck, prepared
in asphalt. When we

feel like top dog we can
get like that, greedy.

Smeared in oil, stuck
in tar for life. TV

dreamed up in southern California,
you made it in southern California.

Home sweet home,
sweet crude, sweet tar.

WOOLLY RHINOCEROS

Coelodonta antiquitatis

I would be offended to be a gorgeous beast, powerful, precise, and to get no credit as the true horned and fluffy hero. Instead of a thick coat, yes, sometimes adorned with burrs, sometimes knotted to hairballs, instead of a match-anything taupe horn, the unicorn was depicted as a sweet shop confection. Body taut and lean, eyes that sparkle like anime. Not a stocky darling on a piece of plywood, instead on bedroom dressers across North America, tepid examples of beauty. Stereotype of idealized girlhood fantasies: a shining horn, porcelain on top of porcelain on top of porcelain layered in glaze and sparkles, whimsy without heart. So sturdy it's said hyperdisease may have killed them all. A supersized disease. Woolly rhinos weren't special one-of-a-kinds, not princesses of the steppe-tundra. They coexisted, mammoths on one side, grazing near their megafauna neighbours. The magical aren't always mythical. Extinction cultivates a cult of worship. And how we should dream of standing on your mud-sticky shoulders, gazing into the distance at the factories that pour out porcelain, to the thrift store shelves soon to be littered with tiny sculptures outgrown, unloved, yet not extinct.

GIANT OTTER

Siamogale melilutra

There is so much to say about you, and yet so little is known. Just start-
ing to explore, not broaching understanding. Naively, I admire mystery.
To know you better my impulse is to ask boring interview questions:
What was a day in the life like? What kind of fish did you eat? If you
could be another animal what would you be? I have to ask where you've
been: Did you live along the shore? Did you hike down at midnight to
fish when the prehistoric moon was glinting off your black eyes, dip
your whole self in the swamp? I have to imagine you fleshed out: Were
your paws like a modern river otter's, confident and grabby? Were your
whiskers as long as you were wide? Did you catch glimpses of yourself
in the dark water and sigh, in awe of your own majesty? No tools nec-
essary, jaws split mollusks like cracking peanut shells. To write a love
letter I have to see the dark side of you: What kind of trinkets did you
steal from your neighbours? Did you hold the heads of the weakest
under the surface? Could you imagine a future where no one knew you
existed, where you weren't lounging, fur submerged in a wetland swamp,
ready to strike?

ACKNOWLEDGMENTS

Thank you to my editor and friend, Nikki Reimer, who is so excellent and smart and gave me the notes I didn't know I needed and those are the best notes of all.

On our third book together I feel so grateful to the team at Talonbooks: Kevin, Vicki, and Spencer Williams. And it was especially wonderful to work with Charles Simard who delivered copy-edits to die for and andrea bennett, a generous talent who made my book look stunning and fun.

Daniel Zomparelli: I fucking love you. For so many reasons, but especially for always telling me to add more jokes to poems.

I can never thank my writing group enough for almost fifteen years of support and friendship and snacks: Sally Breen, Keri Korteling, Nancy Lee, Judy McFarlane, Denise Ryan, and Carol Shaben.

It's not just about the writing part. Here is a big-ass list of people who make my life as a writer and a person so much richer and funnier and better: Roxan Marucot, Jason Bay, Cynara Geissler, Jen Sookfong Lee, Meghan Waitt, Kellee Ngan, Marita Dachsel, Sachiko Murakami, Amber Dawn, Billeh Nickerson, Alana Green, Carleigh Baker, Sean Cranbury, Claire Tacon, Chelsea Rooney, Ben Rawluk, Erika Thorkelson, Gabe Liedman, bobbi mcdonald, Clare Kenny, Travis Borque, Jag Dost, and Elee Kraljii Gardiner.

Wowee. I have so much gratitude and admiration pulsing in my heart for you all. If I forgot anyone it's because I'm a jerk. It's not on you!

Love and thanks to the whole Del Bucchia family: Henry and Teri and Andrew and Helen and Sophia and Cosette, and to Adorando and Loredana who we miss terribly. And more love and gratitude to the Kushners and the Catalanos.

Everyone listed here and all of my loved ones are such a big deal. I hope I thank you enough outside of the back pages of books, but I'll try to do it even more often.

The following poems appeared in different forms in these places and for that I am delighted.

"Marketing" in *Line Break*, an art and poetry blog by *subTerrain*

"Fashion" in *Matrix*

"Boys Will Be Boys" in *Room Magazine*'s "No Comment" project

"All Joking Aside" and "Perfection" in *NewPoetry*

"URGENT!" in *ti-TCR*, a web folio by *The Capilano Review*

"New Rules" in *That One Thing You Said: an exhibit of visual poetry* at Verses Festival of Words

"Jefferson's Ground Sloth" in *The Oddments Tray*

"Woolly Mammoth," "Scimitar-Toothed Cat," and "Glyptodon" in *The Fiddlehead*

"Shasta Ground Sloth" on the *dusie* blog

Dina Del Bucchia is the author of the short-story collection *Don't Tell Me What to Do* and of three collections of poetry: *Coping with Emotions and Otters*, *Blind Items*, and *Rom Com*, the latter written with Daniel Zomparelli. She is an editor of *Poetry Is Dead* magazine, the artistic director of the Real Vancouver Writers' Series, and a co-host of the podcast *Can't Lit* with Jen Sookfong Lee. An otter and dress enthusiast, she lives on the unceded territories of the xʷməθkʷəy̓əm (Musqueam), Sḵwx̱wú7mesh (Squamish), and səl̓ilwətaʔɬ (Tsleil-Waututh) First Nations (Vancouver, British Columbia). You can find out more about her at: dinadelbucchia.com.

PHOTO CREDIT: Sarah Race Photography